MMA x NBA

MMA x NBA:
A Critique of Modern Sport in America

Royce Alexander White
with A.J. Barker

CONTENTS

"Pride goeth before destruction, and a haughty spirit before a fall." – Proverbs 16:18

MMA x NBA:
A Critique of Modern Sport in America

by Royce Alexander White & A.J. Barker

0

PRELUDE

With my announcement that I have transitioned into the sport of MMA, there are undoubtedly questions left lingering that the purpose of this book is to answer. Chief amongst them: Why are you not continuing to pursue professional basketball? I have a host of reasons for why this change came about and a sequence of answers that took time to develop, (and more time to lead to the change that is now playing out in me). I did not have these answers all at once, nor did I leave at the first reason to leave. But, when I had stacked enough reasons on top of one another so as to move the entire inertia of my being in another direction, then it was almost as if it was no longer a question of whether I stayed or went, it was rather a question of "to what do I turn next?" The final direction of that answer was "to MMA", as is already evident, but there is much to cover prior to that ultimate resolution.

More than anything, the bigger questions of sports, development, and their relation to society have been like knots in my psychical muscle demanding release, confounding my development so long as they remained unattended to and unanswered. 'Purpose' is a universal question, though I'm not directly addressing that here. These *sports purpose questions* I have just laid out (one's development, the relation of sport to society) are what I would call a form of '*applied purpose*' to the realm of sport. I am not seeking to answer *here* the universal question of purpose, in an existential, psychological, philosophical, or religious sense; instead I am seeking to answer the question of purpose in an entirely proximal and narrowly defined practical sense: in relation to the world of sport. I'm doing this, most of all, because I have formed a sort of intuitive sense that the proximal and practical dimensions are the right locale in which to answer the question for the most people, or for each of us for most of the time of our lives. If here I am still wrong, what is then left is the acknowledgement that the narrow and practical sense is where I am best suited to engage with this question at this time in my life, and to the limits of this point in my development, being still aged only 27 years. I have much of my adult life left to acquire the fundamentals, skill, intuition, and mastery necessary to more aptly address the larger question of purpose in the truly universal sense: so shall I do.

All things in due time.

1

GATEKEEPERS

I.

The most visceral catalyst in me to give a hard "no" to basketball lies in the question of gatekeepers: it is that primal desire to say "no" to those trying to stand over us, as mere persons, ruling over our entrance or denial into their field of pursuit. The NBA is infested with gatekeepers at every level of its operation.[1] It's debilitating to the spirit wanting to pursue something and being kept out by mere intermediaries, not intermediaries that are themselves subject to the fires of the field, but ruling in favor or against you participating in it from a safe and untouchable distance. For them to sit

---

[1] *Comment:* (And all the mainstream American professional sports leagues.)

there and say "no" to you by their decree, with no possible path to appeal, does more than disappoint: it shatters your belief in merited authority, in the motives of people in general, and in optimism for the future -- both your own and that of the larger society. *(It is not to justify those impulses, but to clarify them)*. Like anyone else though, we go on living and we try to point our pursuits in another direction, sometimes -- and even often -- bitterly, but nonetheless it's what we do. In the mind of a competitive team sport athlete like myself, the green pastures of individual sport and the open access to them lies there like a utopian dream providing all the solutions to your current concerns. And so naturally this whole process in me toward Mixed Martial Arts has been in part or in full motivated by that gatekeeperless mystique of individual sports. In individual sports you're not *drafted*, nor are you hired or fired by a coach or general manager. In that wild west, libertarian sportscape of individual sports, you're on your own. Does not the true competitor long for just that?, the opportunity to be exulted or condemned solely on their own merits or demerits?

And so we can see that from the beginning the draw of individualized sport held an opportunity and a freedom that hyper bureaucratized team sports never could.

II.

There's something deeply personal and humiliating having to look a 60 year old man in the eye as they tell you that you don't have what it takes to compete in the sport of their oversight, having shockingly little to do with your ability and much more to do with your personality and disposition. The psychological dynamic of idealization-devaluation plays out in spades in professional sports. They fawn over some idealized image of you and your "potential" one second, and then the next they devalue and reject you out of hand. It's a symptom of psychical disorder, characteristic of a dysfunctionally developed adult personhood. It's where first you idealize a person, making them not a person but an unsustainable idol of sorts, a collection of projections and wish fulfillments; and then second, (the real detriment of the idealization mechanism), as the person inevitably disappoints you to your unrealistic standard, you flip to devaluing them, where they are worthy of contempt and hostility, something to be cast aside and discarded. The worst part in it all is that they use you falling short of their idealized fantasy to vindicate their compulsive polarization toward devaluing you. It's impossible to survive or grow through.

One of the realities of dynamics such as these is that if you are in a sufficiently large enough group of people, the idealization-devaluation won't manifest itself in the locale of a single individual, rather it will fragment across the whole group, and certain ones of the group will get the singular idealization attitude and other certain ones of the group will get the singular devaluation attitude. The fragmented dysfunction of the psychologically prepubescent person sows disorder and reaps destruction both direct and collateral, stunting the growth in both the idealized and the devalued individual indiscriminately.

For those under the dominion of an idealized-devalue-ing person, in a relatively focal role, what do we do but inevitably change our whole vector of interest toward another direction and another pursuit? What do we do when one person in a gatekeeper position gossips and slanders your name so that everyone else in comparable positions in their field blacklists you as well? -- I'm aware that we wish this didn't happen to us... I'm aware that we all dream of being immutable and unflappable, (and likely some people are more so than others -- that's not mine to discern). But in reality I suspect we all share the fate of confronting periods in our lives where we don't just run up against our limits in a brief moment, but are thrust past them, and held in that overdrawn place for an extended and seemingly unending period of time, until we inevitably find ourselves carving out an entirely new path and chapter in our lives: this book marks just such a phase in my own life.[2]

III.

To begin to understand the dynamic that's at play in our modern corporate and monopolistic sports landscape, an imagistic analogy is helpful. The in-vogue analogy of slave-holder is defunct on many

---

[2] There will be structural and league organizational practices that I will address later in this work to fill out the picture. It's not only an isolated psychological phenomena, there are practical things that I surmise have radically disincentivized healthy player-coach, player-management relationships... I will spend an extensive amount of time addressing those dynamics and realities in the later chapters.

levels [3] if you ask me, far more appropriate is an analogy to cartel leaders, or mob bosses, or mafioso organizations. Why? Because unlike the slave - slaveowner dynamic, in which the slave does not even choose their entry into that world, the athlete does choose to submit themselves toward that field, much more akin to a mobster - mob-boss dynamic. And even just as the mobster may feel that such a lifestyle was little of a choice, and far more something they had to do, by force of circumstance, so too the athlete will immediately realize how little choice they have in pursuing the field of their God given gifts the moment they suggest going another direction. If you're 300+ pounds and can make millions of dollars pushing people around on a football field, how could you not do that? If you're 6'11" and can get drafted onto an NBA team, also making millions of dollars, how could you turn that down? What reason could you have to justify turning away from millions of dollars? Do you have any idea how much practical value millions of dollars actually have? How much tangible value they have? How

---

[3] *Comment:* Misusing the image of slavery trivializes slavery. I don't think that's a good thing to do.

much opportunity they can offer? How many doors they can open? How many of your loved ones you can help to take care of? It really is hard to look at turning away from that as anything short of egoism or pathological martyrdom. I know your health and wellbeing matters, and the people close to you will support you in word if you choose to go another route, but both they and you will undoubtedly sit there confused as to why that couldn't be pursued alongside the acquisition of the millions of value-laden dollars. There's really not some profoundly good answer to that, and that's precisely why any athlete considering such a move struggles to do it. You will be scrutinized for what you do, and much of the scrutiny will be justified.

The coercion in the field of sports is participatory in a way slavery was not, the payment is far greater in both monetary currency (in which being a slave there was none) and a *currency of pride*[4]. The subjugation of the player, like in the mafia or the cartel, is far more erratic, more deceitful, more self-deceitful, and by consequence,

---

[4] *Comment:* It feels so euphoric being a top level athlete, especially in the idealized-devalued societal psychostructure of our contemporary time. The pride gained from being a pro athlete is a currency itself...

uniquely elusive and duplicitous[5], being that it originated from a free-participation landscape. The slave owner doesn't have to be deceitful in their means, -- except for for moral and self-reflective reasons (wanting to look at themselves in a better light than they warrant), because their position and their oversight is secure --, the mob boss or cartel leader has to deal with a moving and movable constituency: their security is fundamentally insecure, and so they have to achieve security through a more psychological and financial influence, one that takes on the veil of participation...

Here's a practical reality that begins to depict this mafioso-like image: The collective bargaining agreements of the major American sports leagues divvy up the revenues roughly 50-50 between players and owners. Leagues that have roughly 30 owners, and 15x, 30x, 50x that on the players side, account a 50-50 revenue split as parity. But with that cursory overview we can't suffice to end this observation right there, on that most sur-

---

[5] *Comment:* Since we played a role in choosing it we have to fight the external obstacles of coercion from other people along with the internal obstacles of self-politicking and guilt avoidance, which can be nearly impossible to uncover and identify, much less effect; all of which creates a uniquely human form of bondage.

face of levels, for that would be cheap and ridiculous, and wouldn't produce even an inkling of where the sport landscape could more reasonably go. It's not so easy trying to adjudicate where money should go and how it should be distributed. The reality is an individual owner, who is only one person, really does warrant a disproportionate slice of the revenue pie from the revenue granted to the individual employee, who is one of many. They brought the whole operation into existence and provided a template on which increased modes of revenue-generation could occur -- in plain english: it's not so simple as to say that the value they added through their field would be there without them no matter what in our society; and actually it's exactly *not* that: without the first order generators (the owners), whole domains of added value disappear, not to be replaced. That "0 to 1"[6] generation the owners in any field are responsible for warrants a disproportionate income. It does... The flaw lies not in those fundamentals, but in the implied assumption that comes with being an owner: that your value and slice of the revenue pie is mediated

---

[6] Allusion to Peter Thiel's book titled "Zero to One".

by *competition with other owners.* An equilibrium approximating an appropriate value distribution is theoretically mediated by free market competition. And much economic research has shown this to be the case........*when the market is actually free.* In the professional sports leagues of America, a set of systems has emerged in which there is *no competition between owners*[7]. In this economic sense, they have literally established a cartel monopoly.[8] They've colluded in the open to ensure that their 50 percent revenue take is not challenged on any side. And like any mafia or crime syndicate, the opportunities for competition are false opportunities; the protections are false protections;: racketeering is the foundational driving product they're dealing in. -- If we were to try to equalize this balance from outside sources, by introducing new leagues, for example, it would be a failed endeavor from the start: To try

---

[7] *Comment*: Anti-competitive measures and mechanisms have degraded the entire sportscape of America -- later we'll show how that anti-competitive plague has seeped into the players and the sports themselves, not coincidentally as I'd argue.

[8] "Cartel", in its technical definition, is, and I quote directly from google dictionary: "an association of manufacturers or suppliers with the purpose of **maintaining prices** at a high level **and restricting competition**." [emphasis added by me]

and erect a competing professional sports league at this point is undercut by the overwhelming market share dominated by the current pro sports leagues in America that consolidated into the purview of single institutions.[9] In such a case as the one of the American sports world, to introduce parity would require not the introduction of alternative leagues, but a direct dismemberment of the currently established leagues... -- I laugh at the thought of how clear this situation and course correction is, because there's no chance this would go over smoothly, or go over at all! Like mob bosses, there's no way they would cede a single inch in this discussion. And so I'll point out up front that the intention of this book is to clarify the situation so as to raise the awareness of the members of our society, not to effect the change, of which I see no hope for in practical reality, as too much self-interest (on the part of the owners and their affiliates) is concentrated toward a single agenda to treat any serious resulting discussion as serious at all. Just the thought of them coming to the table over such a discussion presents itself as a satire in my imagi-

---

[9] Note: We'll touch on the anti-trust dynamics of this process later on.

nation, a story line only Will Ferrell could properly portray in character, magnitude, and theatrics.

IV.

All these considerations began working in me to catalyze my transitioning to the world of Mixed Martial Arts. But why MMA specifically still has to be resolved. The deeper and more prolonged look at the status and dynamics of sports, and then that of sport-enterprise in America, (contrasted against our own history and the current climate of sports and sport-enterprise outside of America), is still to come.

May you be left with a vivid and profuse image of sport in America!

2

GENRES OF SPORT

I.

If we're going to take a serious look at sport, the first thing we have to do is start by distinguishing and categorizing different types of sport. Let us do this by contrast, (through contrasting the different types of sport), so that we can better familiarize ourselves with what constitutes sport, (and then arrive at a more functional working context for understanding sport). Doing this was not what lead me to choosing MMA, but rather, it clarified for me after the fact why I found myself instinctually and fervently pursuing MMA and not something else.[10] I was inspired toward MMA, and only later

---

[10] It was a *Confrontational Sport* (see next section) while also being an individual sport. A rare and ideal combination.

reconciled *why that might be*. From this initial contrast we'll start to develop the tools to also later see the cultural and institutional sport landscape more clearly.

II.

In the taxonomy of the species "sport", there are two sub-species: *direct opponent* sports and *indirect opponent* sports; what I call the difference between *Confrontational Sports* and *Podium Sports*, respectively. In the first class (Confrontational Sports) are sports in which your success is based on how well you do facing a direct opponent, a 'defender', who is actively trying to suppress and interfere with, in a physical and explicit manner, what you're doing; the second class (Podium Sports) are sports where your competition against others is not in the form of direct opposition, but them attempting to execute a similar function alongside you, parallel to you, without either of you ever directly intersecting or interfering with one another -- they are 'defenderless' sports. The Confrontational Sports would be things like: Basketball, Soccer, Football, Hockey, Baseball, Tennis, Lacrosse, Boxing, MMA. The Podium Sports would be things like: Golf, Run-

ning, Swimming, (Racing), Gymnastics, Figure
Skating, Dance Competitions, Snowboarding,
Skiing, Extreme Sports, Rock Climbing, etc. If we
wanted to be flippant and provocative, we could
more generally refer to these as *Sports vs. Activities*,
though that's not necessary, as the direct/indirect -
opponent classification more appropriately disting-
uishes them anyways, but I digress... Most of these
sports in either class can come in team or individual forms, though more generally, Confrontational Sports coalesce with teams more naturally,
and Podium Sports break down into individual
competitive units more naturally.[11]

    The first point in distinguishing between
these two macro-genres of sport is to point out that
evaluations of success are fundamentally different
within the two contexts: in Confrontational sports,
your success/failure is defined entirely in relation
to what you do/don't do to your opponent. It's
technically relative. We don't have an absolute
scale in which we even attempt to appraise success,
nor would it be fitting for us to do so. What matters
in the end is how you execute a predetermined aim

---

[11] MMA being an exception. It is both *Confrontational* and individual.

(scoring a goal, basket, touchdown, point) against a competing person directly trying to stop you from being able to do just that (these are sports where you face a defender), and the winner is not the one who achieves a certain preset amount, but simply the one who more successfully performs the point-scoring goal better than their direct opponent... In podium sports, by contrast, you set out to execute an action that is measured by a codified system of appraisal, are given a score for what you do (either points earned, or time completed in) and are then ranked after the fact in comparison to other people, indirectly, who tried to do the same thing in a parallel effort to your own. The scoring system is absolute and not relative... In Confrontational sports, they're dichotomous, and there is a winner and a loser. In Podium sports, they're multiplicitous, and the contestants are ranked at the end from first to last, easily allowing for multiple teams or individuals to compete simultaneously and against one another.

What we see emerge from these two different classes of sport is a starkly different monetization capacity and reality. In practical reality: the Confrontational sports are much more easily and robustly monetizable than the podium sports.[12] On top of that, the combination of monetizability and team-formation proclivity in Confrontational sport creates an incentive to institutionalize their sport landscape in both the vertical and horizontal dimensions: we create institutions vertically as single team institutions (The Boston Celtics, The New York Yankees, Barcelona FC, etc), and we create institutions horizontally as cross-team governing bodies or league institutions (NFL, NBA, MLB, etc). In individual sports, there is no vertical institutionalization: the most you get is horizontal institutionalization to govern the oversight and regulation of protocols for the sport and its competitive standards (PGA Tour, UFC, different Olympics Committees, etc).[13]

---

[12] There could be many reasons for this. Some psychological reasons for why it may turn out the way it does, though I'm only speculating, could be: the tribal character of identifying with a team; the cathartic release of domination and conquering; the excitement of multiple humans meeting at a point of contact and getting to witness the fireworks... For the sake of this piece we'll suffice to say simply that *it is the case* that they have to this point produced far more revenue generation and superstar creation than the Podium Sports. Nothing else needs be definitively resolved beyond that here...

[13] With the exception being that there is team formation and vertical institutionalization in individual sports for things like Olympic teams.

However, in any individual sport, whether Confrontational or Podium, (notably different from team sports), there is the immediately viable option of setting up *exhibition contests* between one or more individual parties and competing extra-judicially, without approval or oversight from the horizontal institutions: These exhibition contests even have the real possibility of generating *more* lucrative income than their institutionally oversighted 'league' counterparts.

All this is important to lay out because the insights and criticisms we offer throughout the rest of this work are going to be very relevantly shaped by this exact distinction in the culture and climate of certain sports versus others. An observation of a *Confrontational Sport* dynamic / corruption / dysfunction / opportunity / or vulnerability is going to likely be significantly or even totally invalid to *Podium Sport* application, and vice-versa.[14] This is because the nature and situation of the institutions pervading the one genre of sport are going to be different from the other. Insights we can develop

---

[14] In the confines of this work, we will only be looking at comparisons and contrasts between Confrontational Sports... A treatise on Podium Sports will have to be taken up by another person or at another time.

from differing contexts within the intra-aligned genres (Confrontational sport vs Confrontational sport, for example) will be more relevantly insightful than across genres (Confrontational sport vs Podium sport). Comparing European professional soccer/basketball culture to American basketball culture will be valuable because they are like genres of sport (Confrontational sports), but the one is more decentralized (European leagues), and thereby relies on different systems of macro-competition (ie. Champions League tournaments) than the other (American leagues being centralized and monopolistic). Because of this distinction in league structure, but similarity in sport nature, we have a comparison that is going to be both starkly different and immediately relevant. We'll try to take a prolonged look at what this monopolistic league culture has done to sport in America, and to the institutions and culture of sport in America. We'll also attempt to formulate what sport could feasibly become in America, and what the developmental and societal-wide consequences could possibly and/or predictably be in light of those changes.

In a separate aside note: the absence of conversation around all this is both disappointing and suspicious, and I don't just mean disappointing in a practical sense: it's disappointing in an intellectual sense. It's fascinating *to* think about sport and its applications in this way, and there would likely be a large cohort of individuals who would thrive in 'Sport and Society' theory, or 'sport philosophy', if the template for that investigation and discussion were to emerge. It is my long-shot idealistic hope that a work like this could have a catalyzing effect toward just that. There are intellects in athletes and the world of sport that are hidden from the view of contemporary conceptions of intellect and intelligence waiting to emerge from the darkness of obscurity and the emptiness of formlessness. If this work could be one that is a germ that seeds much further, more robust investigation, explanation, and generation than this one does, nothing could make it a greater success. In my most self-important fantasies and daydreams, *I say only half-comedically*, I would hope it could do just that.

III.

After making this distinction between sports genres and thinking about it, and coming back to it over and over again, it became tangible to me why I loved basketball in the first place, and what was most disappointing to me about the current reality of basketball and why that was the case. I began to see with more clarity the external obstacles, stumbling blocks and booby-traps laid out before myself and many others, and the blacklisting potential in these sports (due to the dual institutionalization, horizontal and vertical -- leading to the infestation of gatekeepers) that breaks the whole spirit of the person being blacklisted. Later on then emerged also the tangible reason why I'm so excited *(almost to an admittedly manic, unrealizable extent, in a hyper-idealized and probably fantastical, grass-is-greener type of way)* for the pursuit of MMA I've found myself in. I can't help but suspect that that same idealization-devaluation mechanism alive in so many of the interactions and relations in our society has internalized itself physiologically as a manic-dejected bipolarized response to our situations in the world.[15] I don't know whether this is a sign of a modern prematurity that used to be mature in times past, or whether this developmental handi-

---

[15] Not to insinuate that it's the only causal factor.

cap is simply becoming more recognizable in wider populations because wider populations are finally being given a voice and a microphone. I suspect it is a combination of both... But regardless of the properly allocated diagnosis, it is undeniably *the case* in our modern times that the manic-dejected physiological response is pervasive.

3

WHY WE PLAY

I.

I remember sitting and watching a feature Kobe Bryant did where he talked about what drove him, and he remarked that primary to his motivations was "a fear of failure". That attribution of his motivation to a fear of failure always stuck with me. I think it was for two reasons: one, I admired the way that he said it, the look in his eyes, the gravity of thought he had clearly given it, the weight it held in him; and two, because I felt that even though he had given it immense thought and it carried much weight, it felt as though there was something subtle in it that slightly but significantly missed the mark... Let me see if I can do this thought justice.

I've always admired the singula
and introspective greatness of Kobe Bryan
be a tough sell to call him the greatest
player of all time, but I don't think there's even a
close second to him being the greatest Athlete-
Genius of all time. Tom Brady doesn't form his
genius into words and composition. Michael Jor-
dan didn't even attempt to have it. I don't see it in
Tiger Woods. Magic Johnson doesn't come close.
Nor even a Diego Maradona, or a Pele; Christiano
Ronaldo and Lionel Messi don't even try to. The
closest examples I can come up with are Bobby
Fischer (Chess), Richard Sherman (Football), or
Bjorn Borg (Tennis)[16], manifesting a combination
of intensity and conceptualization, where everything they say and observe is original and generates
as if from a lived confrontation with the uncom-
fortable truth they've uncovered.[17] Where thinking
is not an effortless background computation, but a
concentrated effort they desperately need to wrestle
with for some ungodly reason to mine out the dri-

---

[16] Watch youtube video: "Bjorn Borg Exclusive Interview in 1985
(English)"

[17] For further reference, Jim Harbaugh (Football Coach) is an example of this disposition in a coach.

ving impulse underneath their thought. Their life is one big philosophical crisis they can't help but play out with every fiber of their being, like a Friedrich Nietzsche of sports and the modern world. And so the only way you can begin to depict their disposition is by comparing it to the Artist-Geniuses and General-Geniuses of all time: a Mozart, a Picasso, a Tolstoy, an Einstein, a Newton, a *Nietzsche*,... a Steve Jobs, an Elon Musk(?)... Everything they do is run through with originality and full and perfect expansion out to the limits beyond those we even conceived were there.

There's an anecdote about Picasso where a fellow painter came to him with his life's work. This other man had spent decades of his highly distinguished career perfecting a particular style of painting and expression. The tale goes that after seeing Picasso, he came back a few weeks later to find that Picasso had produced over a hundred original paintings in the man's style, that he had exhausted all the variations the man had disco-vered, and added innumerable new discoveries the man had never even conceived of. And in all of this, what Picasso did was so true and spontaneous that the man didn't even have an impulse to be envious, that he was filled with a complete awe and deference toward Picasso, seeing right then in real time that Pablo possessed a capacity and originality that he never could, and that it would be gone some day, and so there was no interest in the man in doing anything but appreciating it so long as it was in front of him. Picasso, in the man's total conviction, was indisputably a genius par excellence...[18]

Nietzsche took the aphorism and proclaimed his greatness on account of his realization that nothing could communicate like the Aphorism, like the short, to-the-point statement, that only the rarest of geniuses could pull off. And he did it, par excellence...[19]

---

[18] To be clear: No source for this anecdote. I did not read it anywhere, and the details are of my own creation, for artistic effect. I merely added a narrative illustration to the offhand comment I remember once hearing that Picasso mastered styles in short time periods that other artists had spent their life working on, from I don't recall who. My imagination clearly made more of that data point than the reality of me hearing it once upon a time. I couldn't even vouch for having heard it definitively if I were 'put on the stand' about it... If that comment is from a written document by someone somewhere, I never encountered it, nor did I intend for this story to be anything more than an impressionistic folktale of sorts.

[19] "Whoever writes in blood and aphorisms does not want to be read but to be learned by heart.[...] Aphorisms should be peaks--

Einstein, being shut out from the academic publication world at the dawn of his career, doubled, tripled, and quadrupled down, creating not one, not two, not three, but four transformational papers to the absolute foundations of physics in the year of 1905[20]; they call it The Golden Year of 1905, the 'annus mirabilis' (the miraculous year). Some of the other anni mirabiles to keep him company in history are 1543 (Copernicus), 1666 (Newton), 1776 ('The Liberty Year')... Quite the company to keep!......

I think in our era of sports, Kobe Bryant is that. In no one else have I seen the cerebral impulse more fully realized and wedded to the phys-

---

and those who are addressed, tall and lofty." *Friedrich Nietzsche, Thus Spoke Zarathustra, First Part, Section 7: On Reading and Writing. (1883). Kaufmann translation.*

Tangentially: "To communicate a state, an inward tension of pathos, by means of signs, including the tempo of these signs--that is the meaning of every style; and considering that the multiplicity of inward states is exceptionally large in my case, I have many stylistic possibilities--the most multifarious art of style that has ever been at the disposal of one man. *Good* [emphasis is Nietzsche's] is any style that really communicates an inward state, that makes no mistake about the signs, the tempo of the signs, the gestures--[...] Here my instincts are infallible." *Friedrich Nietzsche, Ecce Homo, "Why I Write Such Good Books", Section 4. (1908). Kaufmann translation.*

[20] General knowledge about Einstein, can be readily accessed on Wikipedia, topic: "Annus Mirabilis papers"

ical and competitive form of a man. When a new theory or style is presented to him, he goes and takes another's life's work and exhausts it fully and adds to it anew in a matter of weeks, not as something he did in one-fraction of the time, but rather as though he somehow crammed a life-and-a-half worth of braintime[21] into a matter of a few earthly weeks, living all the time and effort, *times-two*, in the reality of his being, in the earthly span of a few weeks. Like he had a Dragon Ball Z hyperbolic time chamber where he could go for a year's worth of training, at ten-times Earth's gravity, that only passed a single day in the outside world...

Let us take a deep dive now into this 'fear of failure' motivation proposition.

II.

Why do we play? What draws us to the world of sports?; to the world of Confrontational sports in particular?

To most people these questions present as ones in which one person could give one opinion as answer, another person another, a third a third. To

---

[21] *An allusion to 'spacetime'.*

me it's a question of calculation and proof. It's a question of comprehensible and articulable dynamics. It's a question of proper or improper formulation.

And so more specifically, the question really is: 'Why do the greatest players play?'

We'll use Kobe Bryant's 'fear of failure' motivation as a starting point, but through a thorough investigation we'll end up amending it to a new place altogether.

III.

The Crux

The focal point of Confrontational Sports is the eponymous *point-of-confrontation*. We could also call this the *juncture of confrontation*, it is the intersection point in which two direct opponent competitors meet for the briefest of seconds and leverage is secured and won for one player over the other. The football interaction of wide receiver and defensive back provides a great microcosm to conceptualize it. The Wide Receiver and DB, when the DB is in press coverage, incur the point of confrontation at the line of scrimmage immediately after the ball is snapped and the play begins. The result is that one

player, either the offender or defender, set themselves up for the rest of the play to go toward their
advantage, either attempting to finish what they
started, or recover for what they gave up. As you
get to higher levels, the 'juncture of confrontation'
expands in duration and complexity, often with
each play holding a rapid additive sequence of
confrontation points, even at times throughout the
whole duration of a given play. In basketball it is
the point where the player faces up to the defender,
and all their attacking forces come online and the
dominance and subjugation of one player over the
other manifests itself. In all sports you use team
strategy, movement, deception, and tact to try and
scramble and mix the points of confrontation, at
times wanting them to be known and deliberate, so
that there is no escape, and the pressure and tension of the moment reaches its apex; at other times
you hide and disguise the intersection of confrontation, maybe to blue-balls the famished and con-
frontation-obsessed defender, or to add to the ways
in which you beat them, to log wins in periods of
rest and conservation, all to further maximize the
summation and dexterity of your wins.

The key to this all though is that in this exposition we see the two constituent parts of the direct-opponent competition dynamic: there is a dominator, and there is the one who gets dominated. Both parties enter into the junction of *vulnerability*, the cauldron of confrontation, where the winner and the loser will be definitively forged, the one who subjugates the other and the one who gets subjugated.

IV.

Once we understand that the point of confrontation is synonymous with the point of vulnerability, we actually develop a more apt conception of humility in the greatest athletes. Humility here is not the one who is most self-effacing in their speech, rather, in the domain of sport, the most humble one is the one who most earnestly subjects themselves to the point of vulnerability, making no concessions or qualifications for their past or possible future shortcomings, simply subjecting and earnestly *seeking* the point of vulnerability to forge the fusion of atomic collision, the synthesis of the super-particle, making no considerations for the discarded matter being inevitably flung and discar-

ded from the final-stage product. They'll themselves be the matter that is discarded innumerable
times, and so the question of unfailing victory is
not a question or a possibility at all, and we begin
to see that a 'fear of failure' doesn't suffice to address the dynamics of the situation. Failure becomes the thing one has to open themselves to,
they have to seek out the junction in which failure
is forged. The true competitor does not love to win,
for everyone loves to win; the true competitor longs
for the possibility to lose, only then do they feel
alive!... The logical end of a fear of failure would
be an avoidance of vulnerability.

More apt would be a twofold fear, or
twofold motivating force: a fear of avoiding vulnerability coupled with a fear of the humiliation
that is the result of the domineerance-subjugation
dynamic. The one who is subjugated, who is thrust
under the foot of the other, is humiliated. The constituent parts can be restated from winner and
loser, or success and failure, to the dominator and
the subjugated; to the dominator and the humiliated. The more resonant fear then transforms
from a 'fear of failure' to a 'fear of humiliation'
paired with an obsession for, *nae* an addiction to, the

junction of vulnerability. If it is a stand alone 'fear of failure', or even the more aptly worded 'fear of humiliation', the logical end can still be the avoidance of any possibility of humiliation (or failure). The true alchemical compound of factors that makes the great athlete is an obsession with the creating force of vulnerability and a simultaneous hatred of the humiliation that is guaranteed to result in one person from the forged product of the crucible of vulnerability. In combining these two polar opposites, you begin to see why avoidance of humiliation alone, to satisfy the fear or hatred of it, won't suffice...for then the hunger for the creative force of vulnerability is also avoided, something which the great athlete cannot live without, just as an organic creature cannot survive in starvation.

It requires a tension between two opposing forces: it requires the negative force of not wanting to be humiliated combined with positive force of needing to be subjected to the possibility of vulnerability and loss. Only in this endless push and pull does any possibility of greatness emerge in the lived reality of a single athlete. All human success comes in time, is achieved over time, and so the motivation has to be self-propelling across time. A synthesis of push-and-pull is the only thing that can do this. More specifically: the greatness of an athlete lasts only as long as both sides of this equation can retain their vitality and necessity. The second one or the other begins to subside, the whole system is lost and dies for good.

V.

This competitive dialectic, this push-and-pull, was what I couldn't get rid of, even as I was pushed out of the NBA and later took the self-directed step away from basketball. That tension was still alive and pumping in me. It was as though I had to turn to MMA, it was the only logical conclusion to this dynamic seen through to its ultimate aim. In MMA there is only the point of confrontation. There is tact and deception, but in a much more constrained space. I cannot set a screen, or bleed out in transition. There are caged walls holding my opponent and me in one confined space. All we have is the vulnerability and the confrontation, the winner is not performing some predetermined novel skill, the winner is flat-out the one who KO's or taps-out the other. It is the ultimate distillation of the confrontational, domineerance forging, mechanism. I realized once I was there that I had never yet even entered the true domain of confrontation and competition until I stepped into the octagon. It is like everything before this was but a setup, a pre-cursor, to the true destination in which my heart and my loins pointed. Only now am I even beginning to become the person I always longed to be. Only now am I finding a home for my physical-competitive body, like the Christian who finds Christ for their total and spiritual body.

4

ANTI-COMPETITIVE

I.

It wasn't always the case that sports leagues in America were single institution monopolies. We don't have to go back that far to a time when there was the ABA and the NBA, or the AFL, NFL, and then the USFL. My cursory understanding of Anti-Trust law tells me that mergers and acquisitions are not considered monopolistic when one of the merging companies is on the brink of bankruptcy. If that's the case, and I'm no scholar on the matter, then we wouldn't be able to look at the sports league mergers as any type of collusion upon their inception. So far as I know, the ABA and AFL in particular were facing financial extinction, and so the mergers would not have been illegal at the time. However, this is not a technical history, nor is it a technical proposition for change; I've already noted that the point here is to increase eye balls toward a situation and an idea. The end result is clear: singular leagues came to dominate whole markets, and consumers and performers were forced to go to single institutions to have access to sports. The negotiation power of players was drastically decreased, but also the rules surrounding the sports themselves were effected. In-game penalty standards were liable to change by fiat without any pushback or alternative options. The new found anti-competitive marketplace fostered an anti-competitive in-game product, and it empowered the leagues to do all this without even the semblance of checks and balances. Take note of how defensive rules have changed to exaggeratedly favor the offensive player. The in-game defender, who's already at a disadvantage, not knowing where the offensive player is going, having to mirror them while physically going backwards, was given laws that made it so they couldn't even combat with the body position and leverage of themselves to the offensive player. We see this happen simultaneously in both basketball and football professional leagues. Scoring was no longer something you had to scratch and claw for, it was something you'd be given protections for to ease the access to. When superstars acclimated to these new rules in such a way that they expected foul calls based on these new parameters, and complained when they didn't receive them, the transformation was complete. We became witness to the anti-competition of the owners becoming an anti-competition in the leagues superstars. When the new patty-cake rules became official, the large majority of superstars wanted adjudication and protection according to them. Say nothing of pride and honor, of dignity and will, their attitude was now, a whiny, "Hey! Come on! That's a foul! -- *It's the rules!*"

If we're going to understand the anti-competitive reality, we need to understand the psychological attraction of anti-competition far more than the technical history of how the leagues took the structural shape they now embody.

To start: we have to clarify that the psychological attraction of anti-competition is not an attraction to the eradication of competition or the forms of competition. The actual nature of the psychological impulse is one in which the desire for anti-competition emerges within a paradigm held up and rewarded as if it's competition. (That's a key distinction to make.)... Competition is a very rewarding form of interaction. A psychological mechanism is always anchored in a preservation of, and increase in, a particular outcome. In this case the anti-competitive mechanism is one that is designed to increase ones winnings. The duplicity required of the mechanism arises from the reality that non-competition is not rewarded as competition is. And so the only way for the mechanism to be effective is if it simultaneously preserves the presentation of competition while easing and ensuring the chances of victory. One of the real-world results of this is that you can't set up a system in which you *only* win, lest it becomes no longer rewarded as a competition at all. What you want in reality is for your rate of winning, or rate of ability affirmation, to increase. In this way you can still hang your hat on the fact that it's a competition, evidenced by the fact that you lose. Duplicitously they'd say something like, *"If I were trying to be anti-competitive, wouldn't I set it up so I never lose?"* -- No! Not at all! -- That would not sustain the context in which a win is worth anything. In fact, the only way in which one can try to win every single time is if they strictly adhere to competitive principles and the spirit of competition. In that case, the value of your winning is anchored in the increased excellence that was required for your success.

The anti-competitive impulse is born of initial winners who no longer want to have to subject themselves to the fires of competition any longer: exposure to vulnerability and the possibility of humiliation. Here we see the reaffirmation of the eternal adage, 'pride cometh before the fall.' Even more precisely, we see that 'pride leads to destruction.'[22] The desire for insulation and protection destroys that which you seek the insulation and protection for.

II.

Let us double down on this analysis of the anti-competitive impulse and restate its effects to emphasize this mechanisms significance.

Here, like earlier in the piece, we can divide this concept into two categories to deepen our understanding of it: we can say that there is passive

---

[22] "Pride goeth before destruction, and a haughty spirit before a fall." Proverbs 16:18

anti-competition, in which a person wants competition overtly demolished and done away with, so
that no one competes at all; and then there is active
anti-competition, where the person wants the ve-
neer and spoils of the image of competition, but
wants to insulate themselves against vulnerability
and exposure, the actual crux of competition. The
first is the type that wants there to be no winners or
losers, just participants. The second is the type that
wants to guarantee they can win without notable
contestation. This is the type we've been discussing.
In the context of sports and society, the "guaranteeing of winning" has more to do with preser-
ving their place atop a hierarchy than specifically
guaranteeing they win individual games. The "guaranteeing of winning" is actually more akin to a
"guaranteeing of status", or more blankly: a "guaranteeing of monetary income". The last thing a
superstar offensive player wants these days is to be
subject to physical opposition that increases the
chances of humiliation, of being exposed, of losing
their image of dominance, or of getting injured.
And the owners want nothing to do with having to
compete with other franchises, across competing
leagues, where their position is insecure. It's the pa-

radox of competition: because it's hard to win, the spoils of winning are greater, and because it's hard to win and the spoils of winning are great, it's harder to keep winning once you've won. The spoils wouldn't be so great if winning weren't difficult. The psychological cheat code and draw then becomes clear: you want the most difficult thing to win in, because it will produce the greatest spoils, and you want to do the most you can to ensure you win in that thing as often as possible. Of course, the more you make subversive and duplicitous efforts to ensure that you get to win, the less competitive the endeavor becomes, and the weaker the resulting spoils. *But*, in the case of reality and living within this thing called time, the results of anti-competition (a decrease in the value of winning, and thereby a decrease in the spoils of winning) don't play out immediately, and so you can ignore the consequences of your anti-competitive measures and protections. And speaking more broadly, in the case of large corporations and macro-economies, you can delay the consequences decades down the road, and care nothing for the catastrophic results at all.

Like any impulse paradigm, the *pay-off in the short term and consequences in the long-term* allow you to exploit that temptation without immediate recourse. What we're seeing in our sports landscape is mirrored in our society at large: the successful want to insulate their success, and by consequence the whole market is rotting from within. The instability of our political discourse, the rise in the prevalence of the mental health trinity (anxiety, depression, trauma) in the members of our society, are symptoms of that rot, not the cause of the rot. Yes, people are richer, we have more access to material goods, the audience for sports has broadened; but each of those things are readily explained. We don't have more access to the three markets that are most signifying of prosperity: homes, healthcare, and education; we actually have *less*. The audience for sports has broadened because of the broadening of global access to the internet and media: it's more possible for more people to watch. This allows sports leagues to inflate their sense of productive success, like a new Enron, citing hollow ratings and merchandise increases in total quantity[23]. At the core of this anti-competitive para-

---

[23] Though even by that measure ratings are declining.

digm lies the true source of our societal rot. How is it that more people play sports, and yet the professional product has become more muted and stale? ...Even corruption is a symptom and not the cause: the cause is the anti-competitive impulse!

III.

Understanding a psychological mechanism does not ease the practical reality of countering the mechanism. You may be able to formulate the counter-structure to that mechanism, (in this case opening up the league to multiple league competition, allowing fans to communicate their approval or disapproval by which leagues they choose to follow and patronize, etc.), but the real difficulty, as with all psychological realities, comes in the living out of the counter-structure reality you are newly confronted with. The whole difficulty of this pro-competitive landscape, in sports and society, arises in the actual increase in vulnerability that emerges, the actual discarding and replacing of those at the top. The greatest fight back you'll ever encounter will come from a billionaire at risk of losing their fortunes, as they have more resources they can exhaust in their counter-fight. And the masses can't devour the wealthy in their society without radical destabilization ensuing. The true torchbearers must be the superstars and the owners themselves. As with any psychological mechanism, the true resolution must come from within the person themselves. Only self-imposed humility can stage a fight against pride, no amount of societal consensus or pressure can do that. Only superstars desiring to sanctify the spirit of competition can preserve the competitive integrity of the played game. Only owners desiring to compete with owners, desiring to foster the greatest excellence their product can manifest, for the sake of excellence itself, can effectively produce a cross-owner competitive framework where leagues decentralize and are subject to the fires of vulnerability.

The problem always arises after-the-fact, when the increase in these principles produces actual losers. When the franchise owner is staring down the collapse and folding of their failed venture, when the superstar is being exposed for possessing a regrettable mediocrity.

The psychological mechanism is almost never a simple solution. The difference is that it's a solution that requires the will, not the understanding. And the one thing pride and the human mind hates most of all is a solution that is boring and dependent on repeated effort, something that can't be solved or streamlined.

The greatest roadblock to virtue is not ignorance, but defiance.

Defiance is a function of the will.

So too enlightenment is a function of the will.

IV.

Now all this being said, it doesn't mean that everywhere in society competition has to be the answer. Nearly all the areas of regular society are not zero-sum games. However, in the case of sports, the paradigm is, humorously enough, *actually a zero-sum game.* The predicament here is whether we further insulate and assure our great players incontestability, or whether we increase the confrontational potential and foster the exposure to vulnerability, thereby sanctifying the competitive framework, (and with that, sanctifying the spoils of competition). The predicament here is whether we further monopolize the professional sports owner-landscape, or whether we make it possible for players to actually negotiate with owners, and fans to incentivize or disincentivize entire leagues by their support of one comparable league or another.

We can't get there without the proper foundational formation of the leagues and the professional sportscape itself. Let us now leave the psychological realm and turn to the practical, structural reality of these leagues and their counterparts.

5

EU x USA

For most of us Americans the European sports
landscape is as foreign to us conceptually as it is
foreign literally. In Europe there are multiple levels
of leagues within countries, essentially with their
Premier leagues at the top (or something of a comparable distinction), and their secondary and lower
status leagues below that. You qualify for a given
status of league through a process of promotion
and relegation (where the bottom teams of each
division are swapped with the top teams of the pre-
ceding division). No franchise has a guaranteed
place in a given league. Different countries have
entirely separate leagues: Italy has a professional
soccer league, Spain has one, Germany has one,
England has one, etc etc. From each of these sepa-

rate leagues the top teams qualify for a Champions league tournament between the best teams, vying to be crowned the champion of champions. It's a lot like our college sports landscape, where there are the five "Power 5" conferences, each crowning their own conference champions, and all of which are thrown into a pool together to play out the NCAA March Madness tournament, from whence the national champion is crowned. What happens in both of these cases, but in this case we'll focus more specifically on Europe as it is a professional sport landscape, is that the governance of the individual leagues is accountable to their own qualification standards, their own rules and regulations, their own roster standards, etc etc. The integrity of the sport is not consolidated into one centralized bureaucratic monolith. This means that whole leagues can experience pushback to the rules changes and regulation changes they make, as players are capable of traveling to other leagues and striking other deals, and fans are capable of turning their attention to alternative leagues where great competition can also be found. The leagues aren't free to impose whatever regulations they want without any threat of defection or diminution of product allegiance. There is no "salary cap", there is no limit a player can demand in compensation, there is no guaranteed revenue share for the owners, there is no draft process that each player has to helplessly throw their name into and hope works out for them in some completely out-of-their-control process.

If we take a second to consider this draft process that American leagues are uniquely employing, we begin to see that precisely this mechanism constitutes the original sin that engenders corruption through every other business and transactional facet of our leagues. Even our should-be virtues are contaminated through the exposure to team drafting.

II.

There's no doubt that our league drafts are some of the most entertaining and exciting events in our American world of sports. The lead up, anticipation, plotting, viewing, excitement and disappointment: it's all fascinating and compulsively addictive to watch and follow. I don't doubt for a second that it is an area of each of these leagues that fans immensely enjoy and for good reason. I wish that I did not have to point my scrutiny at this draft process, for it really is exciting and memorable and produces an overwhelming feeling of achievement, affirmation, and having 'made it'. My reason for turning my attention toward it is not one of any bone to pick with the draft or the presentation that surrounds it; it's even endearing how playful and fun the whole process is... My reason is diagnostic integrity. I can't look at any of the further dysfunctions in the structures of the leagues without the intellectual honesty to realize even more clearly how the draft is the fulcrum on which everything else hinges. Without a correction to the entry process into the league, especially when it's so glaringly flawed as the draft process, there can be no correction to the composition of the leagues themselves.

III.
Drafted

In no other industry would you be forced to enter into it in such a helpless and uncontrollable way. Could you imagine if movie studios got to draft any actor they wanted, and that actor had to do whatever movies the studio decided for them? Could you imagine if writers, or musicians, had to go to the label or publishing house that picked them or not get to be in that profession at all? Could you imagine if politicians were drafted into political parties, and had to represent the views of their drafted party no matter what their own views were? It's ridiculous even trying to simulate such a notion in any other field. What kind of leverage is given to the management of the drafting teams in our American sports world?

For starters, it always matters who our managers and bosses are. The notion that we can transcend the negative and dysfunctional relationships and people around us is the epitome of vainglory and hubris. It matters what kind of relationships we have with them. It matters whether a culture of mutual respect is established from the get go or not. It matters whether you have two sides of a partnership wanting to be there and self-motivated to see it work. Now we all know that we don't all get to have that, and I can't speak of professional sports as though it's the only place where people are in unwanted partnerships with their managers and bosses, it's not. However, I don't think that means that we thereby nullify any reasonable effort to cultivate partnerships that are generated and maintained in a voluntary manner. The standard for improvement can't be everyone everywhere gets improvement or nowhere gets improvement. What we have in the American professional sports landscape is a circumstance in which the foundations of reciprocality are entirely undermined. Let's look at a few of these real consequences:

Personalizing a contract and negotiating on behalf of particularities that each person has or doesn't have becomes impossible. There's no way in which a person can negotiate with the proper leverage of alternative options on the table. Of course any player can negotiate some particulars with the team that drafted them, but true negotiation emerges when both sides can have multiple alternative options available outside of the direct negotiations occurring between two specific parties. The owners are already able to select for alternatives, and we see how in unrestricted free-agency players get to bring that negotiation power to the table in a preliminary way. The maturation of this process would include the possibility of unrestrained salary negotiation, unrestrained benefit negotiation, unrestrained particulars negotiation. The viability of owners through the psychological and relational environments they foster would then actually come into play. Their physical franchise location or brand would no longer dominate the attractiveness or disinterest of a team to free-agents. The circumstance, culture, and relationship could have an actual chance of trumping the brand and market vice-grip that currently dominates the free-agency market. In the current draft and salary cap model there's no process by which a situation designed to be mutually beneficial to player and owner can non-arbitrarily emerge.

Second, dissatisfaction or underperformance is incentivized to be discarded rather than looked into and invested in. With a revolving door of draft options and a guaranteed stream of future player options, it's actually unreasonable for a manager or owner to re-invest in a player-coach relationship that is not operating ideally. I can fully understand that if I were a coach or manager, it would be bad coaching or bad managing for me to *not* discard the vast majority of underperforming or dissatisfied players. We'd have a guarantee that we can pick for entirely new players that following year, *and every year after that*. We can't get relegated to a lower league, we won't have our salary cap expanded or constrained based on what we do, so why wouldn't we discard it and wait it out? It's far easier, and any of the feasible consequences *(being relegated, spiraling the costs and overhead of the organization)* of doing so don't manifest any actual consequences. In any real business, the desire to discard all your imperfect relationships is counterbalanced by the impossibility of having an infinite employee turnover supply. In our professional sports leagues, *they actually have an infinite and guaranteed supply of employees to turnover.* That's a major flaw.

Third, you have a system set up without the possibility of any appeals process. Like the first point, negotiation becomes a facade and any measures to counter a negative situation are ruled out.

Fourth, you increase the blackballing potential that every manager holds. It's the racket of all rackets. You force a player into an involuntary partnership, and then if that partnership doesn't work out, it becomes fodder for the vindication of that player being an untenable and unmanageable employee. It's a complete farce, and like a mobster, they're selling you protection for violence they're threatening. In this case, they're degrading your character based on a partnership that was antithetical to healthy character in the first place.

And finally, piggy-backing on the fourth point, you degrade the values and virtues we most hope to be emulated and demonstrated in a society. Fidelity, loyalty, commitment, contract fulfillment. You create a landscape in which commitments are rightly undermined, and the lesson emulated is one in which commitments and institutions of commitment are discarded as invalid and corrupt -- because they've actually become that. It's very important that when someone makes a commitment that they try to see that out. That's a very important societal value to encourage, promote, and most importantly of all: actually realize. We have a degradation of traditions and institutions of commitment in our society because we've degraded all the tenets that make commitments and their institutions valuable and meaningful. If you eradicate the tenets that make a commitment meaningful and valuable, of course the leftover institution formerly representing that commitment[24] can then be discarded and cynically mocked overall. Once again, we have a

---

[24] Yes, I'm subtweeting the institutions of marriage.

glaring example of a racket. The reason the commitments of professional sports contracts aren't
honored or taken seriously is not because the players have lost the capacity for that virtue, or because
commitments shouldn't be honored; it's because
the player-management partnerships that a person
enters into the leagues on were never structurally
voluntary to begin with. Those involuntary grounds themselves would be worthy of annulment in
even the most serious and iron-clad of marriage
contracts, so of course they're worthy of annulment in an NBA or NFL contract... We can't degrade the values and particulars of our institutions
and then complain when deconstruction of those
institutions ensues. And unfortunately, most of the
people who argue on behalf of institutions are ridi-
culed when they demand that certain axioms and
premises be upheld. The real racket comes in the
form of the people who proclaim that the axioms
and foundations need to be amended, and then demand the degradation of the institutions is because
old bodied traditionalists won't change with the
times and plague the environments of those institutions with hate and deaffirmation. Erroneous! The
parity, spirit of competition, and integrity of our

professional sports leagues isn't under threat because people want to do away with salary caps and encourage free-association and free-entry into partnerships, it's been degraded all along the way by precisely those measures in the first place! We've degraded the structures of the institutions, and now we're upset when people want to either A) do away with the institutions, or B) restore the institutions to their proper foundations..... We won't have a culture of virtue if our foundations are disanchored.

IV.

EU x USA

In a country with 325 million people, with a couple hundred division one basketball programs, and hundreds more spanning divisions two and three, it's funny that people don't openly question why our professional sports landscape only accounts for 30 teams in total. If we add up the number of teams in the top Spanish, French, English, Italian, and German soccer leagues, we get 98 teams[25]. The population of those 5 countries is just over 310

---

[25] EPL (England): 20 -- La Liga (Spain): 20 -- Ligue 1 (France): 20 -- Serie A (Italy): 20 -- Bundesliga (Germany): 18 -- Total: **98**

million[26]. If you then go and start to add up how many teams they have in their second and third leagues (where the aforementioned system of promotion and relegation is in play with their premier / top leagues), you begin to see a professional sportscape that accounts for hundreds of professional teams[27] . The craziest part looking at all this is the realization that -- given how many kids in America grow up playing sports and are deeply passionate about playing sports -- *we're* the ones that are ridiculous for our professional sports landscape that only includes 30 teams per sport. What kind of unnatural, exclusionary, arbitrary class structure are we trying to superimpose onto our sports landscape?? Given the overflow of partici-

---

[26] Populations: England, 54.79 million -- Spain, 46.57 -- France, 67.12 -- Italy, 60.59 -- Germany, 82.79 -- Total: **311.86 million**

[27] England: Premier League, 20 -- EFC Champions League, 24 -- League One, 24 -- League Two, 24 -- National League, 24 = **116 teams**
France: Ligue 1, 20 -- Ligue 2, 20 -- Championnat National, 18 -- Champ. Nat. 2, 64 - Champ. Nat. 3, 168 = **290 teams**
Italy: Serie A, 20 -- Serie B, 19 -- Serie C, 57 -- Serie D, 168 = **264 teams**
Germany: Bundesliga, 18 -- Bundesliga 2, 18 -- Bundesliga 3, 20 = **56 teams**
Spain: La Liga, 20 -- Segunda Division, 22 -- Segunda Division B, 80 -- Tercera Division, 366 = **488 teams**

*Handcounted on Wikipedia.

pation we have in collegiate athletics, there's no doubt that many more sports clubs would be able to be built and supplied here in America than we even come close to having. And if there weren't one monolithic league that dominated and bottlenecked them all, the money generation wouldn't be so lopsided either. In Europe, the Bundesliga, the EPL, La Liga, the Ligue, and Serie A all have billion dollar valued franchises.

Combine all this with our amateur collegiate sports landscape, which actually has a lot going for it, as I'm going to lay out in this next chapter, and we'd have a far more robust sports landscape than people are conceiving of.

6

THE CSQ

The College Sports Question (The CSQ) is one in which you may be surprised to find out that I'm not on the side of reform, especially given how in-vogue it is to lambast and criticize collegiate sports in our current sports commentary atmosphere. There's one primary reason above all that deter-mines my stance: in no system of amateur or farm-system athletics is there any semblance of fan int-erest or revenue generation. If we uprooted the collegiate sports landscape and replaced it with pre-professional age constrained minor leagues, we wouldn't transfer the current revenue going to the NCAA into this new minor league system. Again, there is no evidence anywhere that fans are interested in unaffiliated minor league sports. This key reality informs the most significant aspect of the collegiate sports landscape success: it's paired to college institutions, which bring with them emotional attachments and bondages all their own, loyalties all their own, interest all their own. It is the vast edifices of alma-matership and the missions of universities as institutions of nurturing and education that provide the template in which people are excited and willing to support and endorse them. The reality is that the brand names of college institutions and the filial devotion they receive from alumni and surrounding fans is the driving source of the monetary production that follows in behind them. This means that the actual proper adjustment to make is not one in which the bill is picked up by the universities, but an amendment in which the amateur status of the athletes is eradicated and players be allowed to generate whatever monetary income they can secure for themselves by whatever means they can achieve. If that's through endorsements, or running offseason sporting camps, or giving speeches, or doing appearances or autograph signings, all of these things should be open to garnering income for the collegiate athletes to the extent they can garner such income in the voluntary market. Athletes should also be permitted to sign with any professional franchise at any time, from childhood on up, just as is done in the European professional sports landscape. They should be eligible to play collegiate sports in their sport of choice so long as they have not been on an active roster in a top league competition game of that same sport. Once that has occurred they will then be ineligible to play at the collegiate level, but not before. By opening up the income possibilities for collegiate athletes outside of the collegial institutions you allow the universities to retain their value added that they are reasonably providing while allowing players to capitalize on the value they can produce, either big or small, commensurate to what they can command. In this situation it would not be unallowed for a university to enter into a monetary contract with a player or prospect, if they choose to. There would be no salary cap or guaranteed income, but it would not be predetermined that a university pay their athletes. Again, logically consistent with the aforementioned structural emphases laid out in the previous sections, the income production and mediation would be anchored in its being subject to a reciprocal foundation of voluntary participation and agreement.

II.

We have a great opportunity in America to have a robust sports economy and culture, one that edifies the individuals, institutions, economy, consumers, and values of America. The fact that we wedded sport engagement and participation to our collegiate institutions was a profound move that uplifted our entire university culture and economy in America. It was a brilliant match that enhanced the productivity of both the academic and athletic sides of our youth and early-adulthood culture. It is singularly unique in the world, and it is magnificent that we did so, (and that it turned out the way that it did). We should not throw that away by prematurely and ignorantly monetizing *that* aspect of our sports culture when it is a shining light of pre-professional sports anywhere in the world.

One can't help, when they seriously consider the structures at play, but realize that the efforts to institutionally monetize the collegiate sports landscape are little more than a reactive compensation for an unwillingness to critique any of the structures of our actual professional sports leagues. It would be utterly foolish to demand the university institutions to be compelled to provide additional wages to athletes when there is an actual added value that they do bring to the table: both market exposure and the opportunity for a fully compensated education. In terms of monetary value those are not cheap compensations, (especially if those opportunities can be leveraged in the secondary economic markets surrounding sports)... But that seems to be the spirit of our times: avoid the real and formidable culprit and outlet all our dissatisfactions and indignations on the low hanging fruits and easy targets. Turn your scrutinizing eye toward the professional structures, toward the dynamics of contractual formation and agreement, toward the nature of competition and the incentives or disincentives that act on it. All of this requires actual thought and effort to perform any thorough analysis or accomplish any resolution. And the resolutions can be found.

7

PROPHESY

I.

We're not that far away.

There are three main innovations lying at the foundations of this whole work:

First, open up collegiate athletics to endorsements and voluntary compensation commensurate to what the collegiate athlete could command, regardless of what level they are participating in (divisions 1, 2, or 3).

Second, do away with league drafts and salary caps. Let players earn the value commensurate to what they can secure, and let teams cultivate their player-coach, player-owner relationships to bolster or weaken their attractiveness or disinterest from prospective players.

Third, create league structures in which promotion and relegation is a functional reality, tautening the competitive tension infusing the leagues, improving the product for fans, and further incentivizing player-coach and player-owner partnerships that are grounded in mutual interest and mutual betterment.

All three of these steps are united in their shared principle focus of reciprocating the people-to-people interactions and structures as the mechanism of legitimizing and facilitating the product that emerges on top of them. The key foundation to this all is the insight that the interactive structures directly effect the psychological and practical functioning of the participating members, and so we strengthen the emergent productions by strengthening the psychological and practical grounds on which a system is based. We achieve this via interaction-based value structures and principles. It is by sanctifying the interactional structures through reciprocal principles that we practically effect the psychological and productive functions of the system that emerges from those interactions. In the case of sports, it's not just an effort to strengthen the player-coach and player-management relationships, it's directly tied to the competitive principles and culture that emerges in the actual playing of the games themselves.

II.

And so let us close out by envisioning what the actual reality of sports in America could look like.

Like Europe, it would have to be geographical conditions that divided up the already existing franchises into smaller leagues (with them then adding further organizations to their leagues). There wouldn't be any way of dividing them up non-geographically or you'd bottleneck the top league into an even more elitist and singular league. For starters, we could say that you divide America into three geographical divisions: East, Central, and West. You can go by timezone (with Mountain and Western timezones amalgamated into one division). We'd then have three separate geographical leagues. From there, the organizations that already exist would be put into their geographically designated leagues, and each of those leagues would add expansion organizations on top of that. You would also do away with any league drafts; the scouting and recruiting of prospects for the professional level would commence. Any player would be viable to go to any organization in any league; each league could make their own distinctions of how many geographically originating players have to be on the roster or not. The leagues would form out from there. Owners would have to have actual collective bargaining agreements with their players, where those players would be capable of going to entirely different leagues and owners if they felt the league they were in was out-of-touch or ridiculous. The integrity of the game would be cultivated in the same way by forcing rule adjustments to be subject to approval or disapproval of the fans, where actual viable alternative leagues would exist that they could turn their interest to if they weren't happy with their current league of interest.

Minor leagues (for example, the G League) would be intertwined with the top leagues through a promotion-relegation system where, for example, the top two teams in the minor league win access into the top league, and the bottom two top-league teams are relegated to the minor league for the following season.

What we would see if the sports landscape opened up like this would be a radical transformation in the reciprocality of players and owners, born out of necessity, forced to a more genuine place of equilibrium. Secondary issues like mental health, player conduct codes, player-societal relations would all come naturally under the purview of interest for the owners and operators of each team. They wouldn't be thrust into a yearly draft process from which they could discard their current players and turn their sights toward a predetermined and perpetually guaranteed future supply. That future supply would not be guaranteed in the same way, and so their investment in each individual player would be far more fundamental to each and every deal they make.

And so when we actually start to lay this out like this, the lingering question becomes, "why isn't this the way that our professional sports landscape is set up?" The answer is entirely clear and has already been laid out: this would turn the heat up on the owners and financial backers, it would force vulnerability within and across organizations. Right now we have a marriage between the owners and the superstars of the leagues working together in mutual self-interest to ensure the anti-competitive subtle structures that are alive right now stay alive into the future. It's not simply the owners capitalizing on this; it is the owners, with the help of a clique of superstar fraternity players cosigning their efforts, that is perpetuating the current set up into the future.

What they don't realize is that they're rotting the sport from within, and only after its too late will the whole building collapse under their feet. They'll then all predictably scamper off in their own directions and point their fingers everywhere else but straight within. And it will be as if they had nothing to do with the downfalls we'll all be witness to. That seems to be the signature of the era our world is going through these days.

III.

Given that none of this is reasonable to expect to change, since the corruption and psychological bias is as embedded in these systems as we've shown them to be, I'm left with the clarity of inward vision to realize that the transition to Mixed Martial Arts is where I can actually reconcile and integrate the realizations I've come to. I'm excited to embark on this next chapter in my journey and subject myself to the fires of this new field that are far more in line with the competitive fundamentals and spirit of true sport.

The End.

Appendix

Reflections on
MMA x NBA

by A.J. Barker

When Royce and I first discussed the idea behind this work, I was overrun with thoughts about what I wanted to cover and where I could take this. I not only had thoughts on content that I had been writing and wrestling with for the last five years, I also had stylistic ideas about what could be possible through this project. We were embarking on a rather unique journey. Having a 3rd party (myself) write about another persons life from the other persons perspective was actually not what was most unique here. There are plenty of ghostwriters in all sorts of capacities throughout the writing and creative world. What we were doing here wasn't ghostwriting in the conventional sense though. We knew from the beginning we weren't going to present this book as though the ghostwritten nature of it would be at all concealed, we were going to break the 4th wall of the ghostwriting process from the jump (in an appendix like I'm now writing here). But even more unique was the fact that it wasn't going to be a piece in which I turned to the primary character of the story (Royce) for insight or information on how to write this or what to include. It was going to be creative from the word go. I was going to be writing this more as a fictional first person narrative than I was a stand-in for Royce himself. I knew Royce very personally through our going-on 15 years of friendship, a friendship that has only grown closer as the years have passed. So I had a conception of him that was very objective and littered with reference points and insight. But I wasn't going to be screening with him what I said from "his perspective" or why I said what I said from "his perspective" along the way. I was going to write it entirely on my own, go through the edits and rewrites without him being exposed to where the work was headed or had gone, and only at the end would I present to him what I had come up with. From there we knew he would give his feedback, but at that point we also knew the margin of effect he could have on the piece would be small -- The piece would either be 'greenlit' or cast aside altogether. As there was no pre-published compensation involved, there was also no contractual obligation that we go anywhere with the piece, and also no guarantee that the piece would be read by anyone. It was a book written totally in the dark, anchored only in its idea and mutual interest from the both of us in trying it. Of course with this now being presented to you here, it's self-evident that we both liked it enough to want to go forward with it.

So let me share with you here some of the process I went through to try and shine some light on this all and add some context for the interested reader. There was always going to be two cores to this book. The first core was Royce announcing his move to Mixed Martial Arts, the second core was the philosophical treatise on sport that would emerge out of that. This structure offered a very captivating opportunity from my perspective. The treatise had already been thought out in me and drafted in varying forms over the past few years. It never came to completion though as, now looking back on it, it never felt complete. It felt as though it was missing something. It was too abstract and impersonal. I had the ideas sketched out you see here in this work: the foundation of competition is the point-of-confrontation, the point-of-confrontation is pure vulnerability, a different form of humility (one of action) emerges in this context than what is societally endorsed as humility (one of speech), the goal of competition / confrontation is domineerance, excellence is the byproduct that draws people in. I had that logical sequence mapped out explicitly in my own mind. On top of that I had clear conceptions of where our current sports landscape was making glaring mistakes in light of this structure I had formulated. There was an anti-competitive "problem" that was right there in the open if my formulation was at all correct or on to something. Of course I still can't know that what I'm suggesting is indisputably correct, what I do have is a high degree of confidence in what I've formulated. How? It has strong explanatory power, it makes predictions that can be falsified, and it encourages further investigation rather than stifling any questioning or investigation. The combination of those things let me feel comfortable in the confidence I had around it...

Skip ahead and here I had a pretty special opportunity that Royce and I were playing with. It was resonant to what he was doing (going through a transition to MMA, a big and unknown step for a person to make), and I felt that I had a lot I could bring to the table in depicting such a transition. I asked him to give me some leash, to see what I could do with his story and explain from a completely objective perspective, not being the subject myself. It was itself a sort of falsifiable experiment: if what I said was as coherent and consequential as I thought, it would go a long way in filling in his own picture, if it wasn't, he'd feel an acute sense of estrangement reading someone else trying to explain what's going on in himself.

Well, excitingly enough, after quite some time, and me going through multiple drafts, I presented what I'd created to him. He can speak to his own reactions to the piece as a whole, but one small soundbite I'll point out that really felt affirming was when he came to the end of the "Why We Play" section (about the fundamentals of competition), and me presenting those principles as necessarily leading to MMA as it most exemplifies the circumstance of confrontation and vulnerability, he couldn't believe how I wrote that, how it represented so truly what he had lived out over the past x-number of months, and how resonant it struck him, even though he had never explicitly laid it out as I had. I was ecstatic hearing that, because, like a formula, it felt like I had decoded something that could be understood and applied in an objective sense and from an objective perspective. I don't know if there's a more desired outcome to philosophy and philosophizing a person can reach.

But I also have to point out that the opportunity Royce came to me with in writing this piece was something that greatly enhanced my ability to write about all this at all. I don't think that it was something I could have just inserted my own life into and come out of the other end with. Being that I wasn't writing about myself, it gave me a freedom and detachment that reverberates through the pages. It's very hard to represent oneself when so much of oneself is on the line, and all the real moments in their life are sitting there with them; from a third party perspective I didn't have all that, and so I didn't have the ingrained tension there with me to the degree an actual auto-biographical piece would have. It let me dive into the thought and the ideas and the consequences with almost infinite times more courage. An unreplicable courage really, as it wasn't a courage at all. I wasn't talking about myself, it didn't require courage to talk about another person as them. That meant I had a freedom in front of me that most persons would never have. I had a full freedom to go anywhere I deemed with the piece.

Now like any freedom, I did not want to abuse that, otherwise it would have the potential of spoiling it all. And while I can't be the final judge of whether I did that or not, I like what came of it. The result of me making what I sincerely feel to be a genuine effort not to spoil that opportunity also resulted in an unexpected sympathy I couldn't've premeditated going into this. I found myself relating to him and his story on a much more authentic level, something I've struggled to do plenty of times in the past. If you think it's only distant onlookers who have disagreements about things, think again, those disagreements are often there in people close to us as well, and while we may take more precautions to not cruelly dismantle our friends and loved ones when we disagree with them (key word there being *may*), as impersonal trolls are eager to do, we still have them. Royce has heard me align with counter-criticisms to himself and his story many times over. I can still speak of things I deeply disagree with him on. And you better believe there are things I've done and views I've held that he's vehemently disagreed with, and others close to me as well. It's never a fun thing having people close to us disagree with us, and even feel we were explicitly in the wrong. That's not something you can just write off like you can some distant person who is nothing in your life. And often times relations sour over just such deep disagreements or differences in vision. I've certainly lost friendships and relations over the things I've knowingly done, things that, in light of those losses alone I wish I hadn't done, and no matter how many times people try to reencourage us with some trope akin to "well if they weren't there for you they weren't good friends to begin with", it just falls flat in light of our own consciences that are capable of being a thousand times more scrutinizing than anyone else ever could. I know it's hard when someone lives something out and then people close to you side with the criticisms of what you've done (as I've done to Royce many times over). In writing this piece in the way that we did this, I felt a resonance with at least some part of his journey that was foreign to me before.

Royce assured me reading over this book that there would be people that would be deeply opposed to the ideas about league structures and the anti-competitive impulse and whatnot that I've laid out, and being myself, *often times struggling to imagine anyone could perceive my intentions in any way but the best way I conceive of them*, I gave back an assured, "oh, no, it won't be so bad." Well, of course, as I sit with it as time passes, still before it being made public, I concede that he's probably very right. I'm likely disrupting things that would rather not be disrupted for many people. I don't have a consolation for that. A rebuttal of scrutiny, if I am so fortunate to have produced a work that receives rebuttals at all, for rebuttals prerequire interest and reading, which I wouldn't presume my work to be worthy of, not because I think it's a poor work, but because I, like I imagine others feel as well, doubt myself as the messenger to deliver it in the first place, -- a rebuttal of scrutiny would be welcome and justified if you ask me. Now I also know I should be careful what I wish for, for scrutiny can exponentially grow quicker than people foresee even being possible, and I may be fooling myself thinking my pre-acceptance of scrutiny is any form of humility commensurate to what I can support in faith or goodwill. But nonetheless, I have worked hard to envision many ways in which this piece can be scrutinized, none of which will I be laying out here for the reader to antagonize their critical appetites with. I'm a bit more tactful and shrewd than that.

In the end I'll wrap up this note by saying to Royce that I'm grateful for this opportunity. As an early-stage writer, the greatest struggle I've had is getting my voice out there and getting any momentum going behind my writing and thought. I've been turned down by publications so many times I've lost count, or generated preliminary interest only to have it result in nothing. That's created a gratitude in me for this opportunity that is important for me to acknowledge and recognize. I do think letting me write this piece, letting me step into your mind, letting me use your voice as a cudgel wherever I chose to direct it, requires at least a form of humility I feel a deep appreciation for in you.

Thank you.

And to the reader, it's my hope that there's much you can take from this piece, as I have been fortunate to take much from it myself.

A.J.B.
St. Paul, Minnesota
February 13, 2019